Familiar Ground

Traditions that Build School Community

THE RESPONSIVE CLASSROOM SERIES • #2

Libby Woodfin

with contributions by
Northeast Foundation for Children staff

TEACHING CHILDREN AND TEACHERS

Northeast Foundation for Children
SINCE 1981

All net proceeds from the sale of *Familiar Ground: Traditions that Build School Community* support the work of Northeast Foundation for Children, Inc., a nonprofit, educational foundation established to demonstrate through teaching, research and consultation a sensible and systematic approach to schooling.

© 1998 by Northeast Foundation for Children

ISBN 0-9618636-7-6
Library of Congress catalog card number 97-75662

Second printing November 2000

Photographs: Peter Wrenn, William Elwell, Cherry Wyman, Timothy Coleman, Donna Rivers

Cover and book design: Woodward Design

Northeast Foundation for Children
71 Montague City Road
Greenfield, MA 01301
1-800-360-6332

www.responsiveclassroom.org

Table of Contents

Familiar Ground

FAMILIAR GROUND is a place we are closely acquainted with, a place that we know well. Familiar ground may conjure up an image of the tree in whose branches we spent childhood hours; it may conjure up an image of walking into our own home after a day at work.

Many traditions, described in this book, help children at Greenfield Center School feel that they are on familiar ground. Learning about each other through traditions like All-School Meeting and Mountain Day—with the common language and signals and experiences we share—builds our community. In the spaces where we feel most comfortable we are able to offer the gifts and venture the risks that the best learning requires. We are on familiar ground.

Introduction
The Knowing of Names

THIS SMALL BOOK consists of snapshots of the traditions and ceremonies of one particular school, Greenfield Center School, at one particular place in our history. These traditions and ceremonies reach beyond individual classrooms, drawing upon and celebrating our sense of ourselves as a whole school community. Although we want Center School to be a place where individuals become strong and capable learners, members of classrooms which offer a strong sense of group, we particularly value an entity we have come to call our all-school community.

Community is a such a frequently used word these days. We lament the loss of a sense of community in our neighborhoods. We yearn for the sense of connection that communities brought to generations past. We refer to classrooms and schools as communities of learners, and who would dispute that building community in schools is a lovely and laudable notion? But like many notions, lovely in the abstract, community is hard to define and harder still to construct and sustain in reality. To pronounce a group of people a community doesn't make it one.

One year a group of seven- and eight-year-old students at Center School were preparing to study their town. Their teacher began their study by challenging them to define community. Lots of consultation with parents and other students and references to the dictionary ensued. The next day they shared their definitions and agreed upon the one they liked best: "A community is a group of people who depend on each other for their necessities." The teacher then asked them to name the necessities in their classroom. Water. Books. Paper. Air. A thoughtful list grew as they went around the circle, many heads nodding in affirmation of each item on the list.

"Friends," ventured Sara when it was her turn. The heads stopped nodding. "No way," contradicted a classmate. "Friends aren't a necessity. Not like air and water and books in a schoolroom."

1

Others weren't so sure and votes both ways flew back and forth until the teacher interjected and brought the discussion back to a thoughtful Sara. "Sara, why do you list friends as a necessity?"

Sara thought for a moment. "Because," she said simply, "without them you would die of loneliness."

In a very direct way, Sara had driven straight to the heart of a human need for community. Without friends we would die of loneliness. Yet simply being part of a group does not stave off loneliness. In fact sometimes we feel most acutely aware of our loneliness when surrounded by people. There is a world of difference between a crowd and a community.

A snapshot: A recent time, late in the school year, and our school is coming together for its weekly All-School Meeting. Fragments of enthusiastic, if slightly off key, song float through the opened windows. "Some sing low, and some sing higher..." Groups of students enter the room, join the song in progress, and scout the floor for a place to sit. Shy smiles, broad grins, and silent but gleeful waves are exchanged across the room. Teacher to student, student to student, student to secretary, teacher to teacher. Younger children scramble for older children's laps. Lines mapping the connections made by the smiles and the hellos and the shoulders touching shoulders would show a web of welcome holding us all together in this time and place.

The sense of community is strong, even palpable. But this sense didn't just spring full-blown from being a group of people occupying the same place at the same time. It was built upon many small and specific moments of learning the same verses to songs and sharing traditions, memories of times together and stories often-told.

We begin every year to create our community from essential ingredients like knowing each other's names. Each fall we have a contest, the All-School Naming Contest. Like many of our traditions, it has changed some over the years. When we were a school of sixty, individuals competed to be first to be able to name every teacher and student in the school. Clipboard in hand, people planned time into their days to go from room to room, surveying the faces and practicing attaching names until they felt secure enough to announce at the next All-School Meeting, "I'm ready to try naming the school."

Now that we are a school of almost two hundred, mixed-age teams of students are the contestants rather than individuals. Though the details differ, the rewards are the same. Silly prizes are given, small chocolate crayons perhaps, to the first few teams to succeed. The real reward, however, is the knowledge of each other that we gain. To be a community, we must be able to greet one another, to speak and to listen to one another, to look into each other's faces and note sadness or celebration residing there. And all of it begins with the powerful knowing of names.

Snapshot: A seven-year-old student stands in front of the assembled school and reads a story she has written about a turtle. "Are there any questions or comments?" she asks at the end, a format familiar to us all. Hands go up, and she calls upon members of the audience. "David." "Leah." "Ms. J."

Older children often offer their laps to younger children
at our weekly All-School Meetings.

3

Another snapshot: Jonas is a student leader for All-School Meeting this week and one of his jobs is to ask, towards the end of the meeting, "Did anyone have a birthday this week?" Up go a flurry of hands, and from this sea of two hundred faces Jonas calls the names.

"Andrea. What day was your birthday?"

"Gabe. How old are you now?"

The knowing of names. It is a simple thing, yet from it we build community. If we stop making time for children to go from room to room learning names in September, they cannot recognize each other's birthdays in January. We have learned, over the years at Center School, that, just as we rope off time for math class and time for parent conferences and time for independent reading, we must designate time and create structures which reflect the value we place upon community.

Just as we try to know each other as individuals in our community, we also try to form some sense of ourselves as a whole. In an informal fall tradition we all gather outside our school and form a line, holding hands. It is a fine time to stretch and breathe deeply the glorious New England autumn air. The school year is fresh and stretches ahead, full of promise. We see ourselves gathered, take note of who we are and what we look like as a group. Is the line we form longer or shorter than last year? Is it long enough to encircle our school building? Our building and the basketball court? Just how big are we all together? It is a defining moment.

Some of the defining moments we share as a whole school are light and crisp and glorious. Some are more somber, their lessons harder-won. Along with the sense of belonging that community offers us, it also offers us challenges and responsibilities and obligations. Some weeks we note accomplishments; some weeks we name struggles.

Another All-School Meeting snapshot, this one several years old. First, some background. Anti-Semitic and white supremacist graffiti had been sprayed on buildings, including the Jewish temple, in our town two nights before. Our staff had, at our weekly meeting, grappled with the news. Sadness, outrage, fear,

4

and discouragement hung heavily in the air. Slowly, from the acknowledgment and processing of those emotions emerged a determination to act. We wanted to demonstrate to our students, and to ourselves, our conviction that differences between human beings can be cause for celebration instead of persecution. We turned almost instinctively to a familiar school event—the All-School Meeting—to address the issue. So now, this morning, at our weekly All-School Meeting, three staff members stand in the front of the room before the assembled school. They offer descriptions of themselves:

"I'm old...I'm medium old...I'm young."

"I'm bald...I have curly, black hair...I have straight brown hair."

"I'm a woman...me, too...I'm a man."

"I'm a Christian...I'm a Jew."

"I grew up in the suburbs...I grew up in the hills."

"I'm a single mother...I have no children."

The students listen intently. They love hearing familiar adults sort themselves in this way. One of the staff members concludes the descriptions: "We have many differences. We work together. We like that we are different. In fact, we think that it's important that we are different. Why do you think that is?" The room is silent for a moment; then hands rise, some hesitantly, some with speed and certainty. Six-year-olds and forty-six-year-olds offer their thoughts:

"It'd be pretty boring if everyone was the same."

"It'd be hard to tell who was who."

"We wouldn't have to communicate and talk if we all had the same thoughts."

"You wouldn't be yourself; you'd be someone else."

"In this book I read, The Giver, *people all have the same emotions and it's an awful world."*

The answers prompt another question, this one from a student in the audience. "Why do you suppose some people hate differences so much?" What a question. Profound and thoughtful answers are ventured, while almost two hundred children and adults sit together for nearly an hour paying attention, listening carefully, responding respectfully. We had come into the room, two hundred individuals with as many different experiences and associations connected with the issues at hand. But we leave, one community, having acknowledged that a bad thing has happened and that we believe that there is a better way.

All the knowledge and common bonds we had accumulated—the naming, the greetings, the sharing about pets and families, the birthday songs, the stories we had heard together, the signals we all followed—enabled that meeting. They enable and are enabled by all the Center School structures and traditions you'll read about in this book—the cross-age lunches, the All-School Games, the first week's "Greeters."

Some of our traditions are once a year events; some happen every week or even every day. They give us ways to greet each other, to learn about each other, to sing and celebrate and say goodbye. These events mark our comings and our goings and affirm our common interests in the time we spend together.

I return to a statement in my opening paragraph. This book contains snapshots of one school's traditions at a particular place and time. The traditions continue to evolve. Each year, with its unique set of people and circumstances, brings modifications. Some of those modifications become beloved parts of the traditions; some are discarded before the year's end. Some of our traditions might transplant beautifully and thrive in your school's climate; some might not be suitable at all. We invite you to borrow and adapt any that appeal to you, just as we have borrowed and adapted from many sources over our almost twenty years as a school. The specifics don't so much matter. What does matter is the commitment to make time and space for the hard work and great rewards of an all-school community life. To be part of a group of people who can depend upon each other for what they need is, after all, quite a goal.

Roxann Kriete
Northeast Foundation for Children

Greenfield Center School Traditions

All-School Meeting

Description: Once a week our entire school community — students, staff, sometimes family, and occasionally a special guest — gathers together for an All-School Meeting.

Purpose: All-School Meetings help the community know each other, share in each other's accomplishments and struggles, and have fun together.

Format: All-School Meetings occur weekly and generally last forty-five minutes to one hour. Each month a different class facilitates the meeting. Occasionally this class will choose a theme for the meeting, either based on a holiday, a special event, or a special interest of the class. All-School Meetings include the following components:

- Coming-in song
- Welcome to visitors
- Sharing time
- Special events

- Birthday songs
- Announcements
- Going-out song

ALL-SCHOOL MEETING is the focal point of community life at the Center School. Once a week our entire community meets together to sing, to play games, to tell stories, to create and participate in contests, to acknowledge birthdays, to share our learnings, and to welcome visitors to the school. Occasionally, we use All-School Meetings to celebrate holidays, to celebrate parents, to welcome new students or staff to the school, or to say goodbye. In All-School Meetings we honor our community's stories and people.

Handwritten margin notes:
- Singing Coming Song (teach in music)
- Welcome New Students
- Birthdays
- Good-Byes
- Singing Going Out Song (teach in Music)

All-School Meeting: the focal point of community life at Center School.

The idea for gathering the school community together grew out of our need to know each other and be known, to share the learning that happens in individual classrooms, and to have fun together as a community. When our school was small, we satisfied these needs by assembling daily in an All-School Meeting. As our population grew and scheduling became more complex, we had to change our daily meeting to a weekly event. In spite of these alterations, the main components of All-School Meeting have remained constant. These components include singing a coming-in song, welcoming visitors, sharing work from classrooms, special events, singing birthday songs, reading announcements, and singing a going-out song.

The Coming-In Song

As each class makes its way into the all-school room—a large room used for many purposes including meetings of the entire school—three teachers sit at the front playing guitars and singing. Also singing are several children from the third grade class who are nervously occupying folding chairs facing the in-coming classes. These third grade children have chosen to sing "Peace Like a River" as each class files into the room to find its spot on the floor. Older children welcome younger children onto their laps and visitors settle into chairs set up specially for them. After each class has gotten settled and everyone has participated in singing at least one verse of the song, the music ends and the third grade leaders each raise their hand, the school-wide signal for quiet.

Each month a different class takes responsibility for All-School Meeting. As one of their responsibilities, the host class selects a "coming-in" song and begins singing before the others arrive so that each class may enter the room to music. Sometimes the song is an old favorite; sometimes it is new. The student leaders model for others the important job of singing. All join them in the singing as they enter the meeting room.

A small cluster of students from the host class sit at the front of the room. They have responsibility for running the meeting of 180 students, twenty staff members, and anywhere from ten to thirty visitors and/or parents, and for helping the entire school proceed smoothly from singing through sharing and announcements to the meeting's finish. By giving students this responsibility and treating them with respect in their leadership roles, the teachers reinforce the principle that everyone in the school deserves respectful attention. No matter who raises a hand to quiet the group, everyone must respond with quiet. Regardless of the song chosen, everyone sings. Every person in the

Seventh and eighth grade leaders of All-School Meeting
wait for the audience to respond to their signal for quiet.

community, from a five-year-old to the principal, receives attention and respect.

Chip Wood, a founder of the Center School, explains the reason for giving and expecting responsibility in this setting from every member of the community: "You do it because that's how you want everything else to be. It has enormous generalizing power." When a seven-year-old child stands before the entire school community raising his arm for silence so that he can begin Sharing Time and every member of that community gives that child their complete attention, a clear message is sent that in our community every person is deserving of respect and responsibility. This message is then carried from our All-School Meetings into the hallways and onto the playground. All-School Meetings set a tone for the culture of the school and community. Allowing children to fulfill an important role in the community helps them develop the sense of significance that responsibility engenders. Being in charge also gives them a sense of belonging and an understanding of the role that teachers so often call their own. It helps to establish the culture of the school as a place where all members of the community are valued equally.

Welcome to Visitors

After the all-school room has quieted, Suzanne, one of the student leaders from the third grade class, asks the visitors to introduce themselves. One by one the visitors stand: "My name is Donna Carson and I teach second grade at the Park Street School in Hewitt." When the last visitor has introduced himself or herself, the entire group of students and staff begins to sing our version of a well known folk song, "This school is your school, this school is my school." No cue is necessary to begin singing to visitors. Everyone just seems to know.

Because the Greenfield Center School is a laboratory school for Northeast Foundation for Children, many teachers and administrators visit the school to observe teaching practices, often on Wednesdays, the day of All-School Meeting. Each week the children sing this song to welcome the guests and help them feel they are part of the meeting.

[handwritten marginalia: "This school is your school, is your school, this school is my school — New Student Song."]

[handwritten marginalia: "Share student work, change focus to 'Quality Work'"]

12

Sharing Time

After the singing has ended, another third grader, Josh, raises his hand to quiet the group. He waits patiently until everyone is silent and looking at him. "The Upper Middles have sharing," he says. Six or seven Upper Middles, the term for fifth and sixth graders at the Center School, stand up and walk to the front of the room. One of them explains that they have been studying poetry and have written poems of their own which they will read. When they are through reading their poems, Jesse asks, "Are there any questions or comments?"

Generally the main focus of All-School Meeting is on sharing work which individuals or groups have done. The day before All-School Meeting occurs each week, children from the host class circulate through the school to find out which classes wish to present a play, poem, song, or project they have created. The host class then arranges a schedule based on the length of time each class will need for arranging their "props" and performing and introduces each class at the appropriate time during the meeting.

Sometimes students share projects they have worked on for

A final rehearsal before these fifth graders perform a song they have learned to play on the recorder at All-School Meeting.

months. The seventh and eighth graders, for example, shared their physics project one year — wind-powered cars that they had spent a great deal of time creating. Sometimes one child has something that he or she wants the whole community to see. One second grader, for example, shared the wind-powered car that he made during project time after he had seen the older students share their creations.

After sharing, the students who have presented their work answer questions and listen to comments. Often students will ask how long it took a person to make her project, or memorize his lines, or practice her steps. Sometimes a student will wonder where the presenters got the idea. Listening to their peers, children learn to compliment and to notice others at All-School Meeting. They see people acknowledging hard work and they themselves begin to praise the accomplishments of others. Even the youngest children are able to raise their hands to say that they appreciate the work of another child.

Special Events

There is a bustle in the all-school room as the children from a primary class, the last class to share, find their seats. They are excited and chatty about the play that they just performed and it takes a moment for them to settle. Some stop to get hugs from their moms and dads before they sit down again. When they are seated, Sandra, a third grade meeting leader, raises her hand: "Mr. S. has sharing." As Mr. S., a second grade teacher, makes his way to the front of the room, the chatter among the children begins again amidst wide smiles and a growing sense of excitement.

Mr. S. holds a pile of papers—notebook paper, construction paper, torn scrap papers. "I have the entries," he announces, holding up the pile, "and I have the winners." Again the room is alive with children's voices. Mr. S. raises his hand and waits for the room to quiet.

This teacher has been conducting a school-wide contest, using All-School Meeting as a time to announce the contest, the rules, the progress, and the winners. The challenge has been to estimate the height of the school. The winner will be the person who has provided the closest guess as well as the most clever method for solving the problem. Some children have counted bricks, some have raised helium balloons to the top of the school, some have measured the lengths of shadows, and some have just taken a good hard look and guessed. Many have worked in groups, comparing notes with other children. The entire school has been excited by and engaged in this contest for weeks. Sixth graders have puzzled out math problems with third graders while sitting on the steps outside the school. First graders have sought out eighth graders simply for an opinion on the best way to proceed. The contest has created a forum for cross-age math problem-solving by challenging the children with a fun task.

While special events are not a part of every All-School Meeting, they do add some spice to our normal All-School routine. Occasionally, we even use our All-School Meeting time for a special event featuring a presentation from someone outside our school community. We have had some fascinating presentations over the years including visits from astronauts, dance troupes, singers and mimes. More typically, however, we use All-School Meeting to draw upon our community resources—to celebrate and take stock of who we are—rather than to showcase performances by outside resources.

Birthday Songs

Greg has the difficult job of moving the focus of All-School Meeting from the height-of-the-school contest to birthday celebrations. After Mr. S. takes his seat, Greg raises his hand and waits; when all eyes are on him and the room is quiet, he asks, "Are there any birthdays?" Hands pop up all over the room.

Class member introduces birthday people by name.

School Birthday Song.

Students wait to be called on by Greg. No matter what class is hosting the meeting, from kindergartners to eighth graders, children call on other children by name. If a child does not know a name, he asks for help from a fellow leader or, especially in the beginning of the year, simply asks the other child, "What is your name?" Whoever is called on announces one person who has a birthday that week: "Jessica's birthday was on Tuesday." Jessica announces her age and goes to the front of the room. The birthday children then decide which of five or six birthday songs they would like sung to them.

15

A child raises his hand at All-School Meeting,
eager to announce that his classmate has a birthday this week.

Birthday announcements are special for several reasons. They require children to think about each other and to remember when each other's birthdays are. They also reinforce the notion of community since everyone's birthdays are acknowledged, even parents and staff attending the meeting on their birthdays. One year when a staff member had just had a baby one student stood to announce Tyler's birth. An eighth grade student then called the hospital from the phone in the all-school room and the entire school asked the teacher on the speaker phone what song she thought Tyler would like sung to him. "Joyful," she replied. In a wonderful moment she and her family listened to the sounds of two hundred people singing and welcoming Tyler into the world and into the Center School community:

Joyful, joyful, joyful greetings
We've come to wish you everything
of joy the coming year may bring.
Welcome, welcome to the birthday child.

Announcements

Again, the all-school room is abuzz with excited voices. Birthday songs tend to engage everyone in the excitement of what birthdays mean for children. Miles, the last third grade meeting leader sitting at the front of the room, raises his hand to quiet the group. "Are there any announcements?" he asks the group. One by one he calls on students and teachers raising their hands.

Like all meetings, our All-School Meeting also provides an opportunity to accomplish business in the community. It offers a time to make announcements and give information. "My dog had puppies and we are looking for homes for them" is not an uncommon announcement. The chance to share information is an important part of the meeting; it helps members of the community keep in touch with one another.

During announcements teachers or administrators may also share important events with the entire school. Administrators may announce upcoming fire drills. A teacher may voice a concern that sports equipment is being borrowed and not returned. One time, a fifth grader rose to announce that one of the praying mantids that his class was studying had escaped and could be lurking somewhere in the school. The time for announcements provides an essential opportunity to inform the community of news and events.

The Going-Out Song

When Ms. C. has finished announcing the upcoming eighth grade soccer game at a nearby school, Suzanne, the same third grader who led the visitors in their introductions, concludes All-School Meeting: "The going-out song will be 'When the Saints Go Marching [Out].'" *The song begins with the entire group singing. At the end of the first verse Suzanne yells above the guitars, "Upper Primes!" The second graders stand up and file out of the all-school room, singing as they go. At the end of the next verse Suzanne yells again, "Uppers!" The seventh and eighth graders stand to leave. The visitors leave with the class which they will be observing for the morning. As the room empties, the singing continues, though with much less volume, until everyone is gone.*

17

All-School Meetings are special gatherings, a routine that children know. They know that they will sing, they will share, and they will see the whole school gathered in one place. It is routine; yet it is special because it provides a time once a week when our entire community comes together to enjoy and appreciate each other.

Making All-School Meeting Work

The following contribute to a successful All-School Meeting:

A good physical layout: We sit on the floor in a large, open room. We've found that having clearly defined aisles (we mark them with masking tape) is important to facilitate coming in and out in an orderly fashion and walking to the front of the room for sharing.

Spirited singing: Participation in singing improves if classes practice the songs beforehand. It's also important to post the words (in large, clear writing) for all the verses of the songs.

Well-prepared sharing: Children should practice their sharing in front of their teacher or their entire class before sharing at an All-School Meeting.

Silence before speaking: We use a hand signal to ask for silence and instruct the children to wait until they have everyone's attention before speaking.

Playfulness and humor: Singing and playful contests create an upbeat tone to make meetings fun.

Fun All-School Contests

When selecting the guidelines and rules for a school-wide contest, we choose contests which encourage playfulness, cooperative efforts and creative thinking. While winners are announced and prizes sometimes awarded, winning is not the focal point of these contests and everyone's efforts are celebrated. We sometimes post on a bulletin board what we call "The Fame and Glory Register" listing the name and/or team name of all contestants accompanied by photos taken during the contest and quotes from the children about the contest.

18

A Yearly Contest: "The Naming Contest"

Every fall as school opens, the Greenfield Center School holds a school-wide "Name the School" contest. Children create mixed-age teams with a representative from each age level to work together to learn the names of all the children and adults in the school. Teachers give teams time to visit other classes to learn names, and at recess and lunch teams can be seen trying to memorize names and connect them to faces. A great deal of excitement swirls around the teams and a tremendous amount of affirmation accrues to everyone in the school as they hear their names being practiced and said many times over! The contest runs about six weeks and at weekly All-School Meetings teams attempt to name everyone in the school amid the rapt attention of all.

Family Facts Show

In years past, Greenfield Center School had a contest that ran each week and lasted all year called "The Family Facts Show." Each week, eight school members (children and/or staff) were featured as "People of the Week." They each created a bulletin board that highlighted their history and interests through pictures, writing and memorabilia. Then a panel of "game show hosts," comprised of several different classroom representatives, prepared a roster of questions based on the information in these bulletin board displays.

Two evenly matched, mixed-age teams were created as contestants. These teams, as well as everyone else in the school, studied those bulletin boards with incredible enthusiasm and thoroughness. The teams also spent almost as much time creating costumes for the show! Teachers were often part of the contestant teams and modeled a lively but cooperative spirit in their participation. The playfulness of the contest, including questions such as "Who is Becky's furry bed warmer?" and "Name the color of Eli's beach towel," set a tone that allowed everyone to be comfortably engaged in the competition.

In this contest, first and second prizes were awarded each week. However, the prizes were made by the children on the "host committee" and first prize was often indistinguishable from second prize. The making and awarding of the prizes became as much a part of the fun of the contest as the contest itself. Prizes included funny hats, goofy masks, paper "pencil holders," etc.

How Tall is the School?

In this much-loved Center School contest, mixed-age teams worked together for several weeks to create strategies for figuring out the height of our three-story school building. Measuring and counting bricks, measuring the heights of each room and adding them together, and releasing a helium balloon with a string attached until it appeared above the chimney were just a few of the many creative methods used. Answers were judged on ingenuity as well as accuracy and each team's work was acknowledged at an All-School Meeting.

A contestant in the "How Tall is the School?" contest
measures the height of the stairs.

What's My Line?

This is a great contest for helping children recognize and know all the people who work in the school. Four children from different classes serve as "The Panel." They wear silly masks that cover their eyes so that they cannot see the "Secret Staffer," a member of the school staff who stands nearby. Each member of the panel can ask two yes or no questions to try to figure out the "Secret Staffer's" identity. To make it even more fun and challenging, the "Secret Staffer" is allowed to disguise his/her voice and can even borrow a member of the audience to serve as a spokesperson.

Favorite Songs for All-School Meeting

Coming-In Songs

The following songs work well as coming-in songs for our community. They are songs which the children and staff know well and they have tunes which are easy to sing, making it possible for people to join quickly in the singing as they enter the All-School Meeting. For each one, we've listed a source for the words and music.

Peace Like a River (*Rise Up Singing*, A Sing-Out Publication, p. 195)

Sandwiches (*The Books of Kids' Songs 2*, Klutz Press, p. 8)

All My Life's a Circle (*Rise Up Singing*, p. 222)

Garden Song (*Rise Up Singing*, p. 52)

Puff the Magic Dragon (*Rise Up Singing*, p. 175)

Going-Out Songs

These songs work well as going-out songs; they are spirited, easy to sing, and easy to modify so that we can easily substitute class names when dismissing an All-School Meeting (for example, *the Prime Reds go marching two by two, hurrah, hurrah...*)

The Ants Go Marching (*Wee Sing Silly Songs*, p. 40)

Poor Howard's Been and Gone (*Folk Singer's Wordbook*, Oak Publications, p. 63)

She'll Be Comin' Round the Mountain (*Rise Up Singing*, p. 177)

He's Got the Whole World (*Rise Up Singing*, p. 209)

When the Saints Go Marching In (*Rise Up Singing*, p. 213)

Birthday Songs

We like having a repertoire of birthday songs for the children and adults to choose from. These have become our favorites:

"Plain Old" Happy Birthday

Chorus to Birthday Cake (*Rise Up Singing*, p. 222)

This song is also known as "Cut the Cake" although we call it "Rock and Roll" and add two fast claps after each "Happy Birthday to you."

Chorus to Circle of the Sun (*Rise Up Singing*, p. 107)

For this one, instead of singing "babies are born," we substitute the name of the person whose birthday it is.

Joyful (This song came to us from the Bruderhof Community in Rifton, NY.)

- Change format of Terrific Kids
- Focus community building and modeling "Quality Work"
- Break School into cross age learning communities to cut down size of assemblies.
- Classroom hosts the assembly - students take charge.
  - Sing Coming in Song.
  - Welcome Song or Cheer to new students.
  - Birthday Song
  - Going out song
- Contests?
- Classroom Buddies Lunch

All-School Games

Description: During All-School Games, children of different ages play organized games together in pre-arranged groups of eighteen to twenty students.

Purpose: This event provides a time once a week for children of different ages to have fun together and get to know one another. It also provides an opportunity for teachers to get to know students in other classrooms.

Format: Once a week for half an hour at a scheduled time, students go to the room of their All-School Games teacher, and from there the group goes outside to play games. Teachers choose games that are appropriate across a broad range of ages. All-School Games include the following structures:

- The school is divided into groups of approximately twenty students each, with each group including children whose ages range from five to fourteen years.
- Games chosen are appropriate for mixed ages.
- Older children are paired with younger children.
- Each group meets at a "home base" classroom during All-School Games period.

ALL-SCHOOL GAMES take place during a half-hour period once a week when children of all ages play together in groups of eighteen or twenty students. At Center School each group generally includes two children from each class in the school. All-School Games include the following components: games appropriate for mixed ages; mixed-age partners; and a "home-base classroom."

Games Appropriate for Mixed Ages

"Help! Help! Free us!" Children hold hands in a line that stretches from the cone that designates the "jail" as far as it can into the enemy team's territory. Members of their team bravely race toward them trying to free their captured teammates. Others, some in pairs with kindergartners, race toward the flag trying to outsmart the flag-guard, a third grader. Still others are playing defense, staying on their own side of the line, capturing the other team's infiltrators. Children scream happily and run in every direction. Finally, a second grader who has walked through enemy territory virtually unnoticed grabs the flag and runs as fast as she can with five children almost twice her size chasing her. When she gets safely across the line she throws the flag in the air and is swarmed by her teammates who give her high fives and pats on the back. "Nice job, Jessica" and "good running" echo from the playing field.

Capture the Flag is an old standard during All-School Games at Center School because it meets all the necessary criteria for mixed-age fun. Children of all ages love it and almost everyone knows how to play. It abounds in opportunities for teamwork and for success. The variety of roles makes the game particularly appropriate for mixed ages playing together. While some positions

Children of mixed ages begin to play
an "old favorite" game, Capture the Flag.

require little running, others require speed and endurance. Freeing one person from jail can be just as rewarding as capturing the enemy's flag. The game requires no skill or strength and is not dangerous.

It is important for teachers organizing all-school activities to plan games that will work with a mixed-age group. Playing basketball may be a fun activity for second graders and it may be fun for eighth graders but putting these ages together to play might be disastrous. Injuries might occur and second graders would probably not feel very successful. One of the main goals of scheduling All-School Games is to give children of different ages and sizes the opportunity to have fun together and get to know one another in a new context. An inappropriate choice of games can hinder this process. For a good selection of games that work well with a wide range of ages, see our recommendations at the end of this section or consult the books, *The Cooperative Sports and Games Book* (1978) and *The Second Cooperative Sports and Games Book* by Terry Orlick and *Everyone Wins* (1990) by Sambhava and Josette Luvmour.

Partners

Robin, a kindergartner, and Jill, a sixth grader, run off hand in hand to get in position for the start of the game. Their All-School Games group is playing a game called "silly soccer." It resembles soccer in the sense that competing teams attempt to score a goal but it is silly because there are three goals, three teams, a huge, light-weight ball, and very few traditional rules. Robin and Jill are running around enthusiastically, kicking the ball and defending their goal. Like other pairs of children, Robin and Jill stick together throughout the entire game, holding hands. Jill is really helping Robin understand the game and Robin likes having a new, older friend; this is apparent from the big hug Robin gives Jill when the game is over.

Pairing younger and older children during All-School Games helps younger children get used to the group and learn the rules of whatever game they are playing. Younger children also appreciate the camaraderie of having an older buddy. Frequently these friendships carry on outside All-School Games time. It is not uncommon to see kindergartners wave to or hug older children who have helped them in a game. Partnerships also give older children a sense of their importance in the group. Being asked to pair up with a younger child lets the older child know that he is valued and respected by his All-School Games teacher. Older students model good behavior to younger children because they know that they serve as an example.

Older "buddies" help the younger children feel more secure and relaxed.

A "Home-Base"

Mrs. L., an assistant teacher in the fourth grade classroom at Center School, walks into a primary classroom in search of a stapler. Flora, a kindergartner runs up to her with a big smile and throws her arms around her. "Hi, Mrs. L.!" Flora says, beaming. When Flora's teacher asks how she knows Mrs. L. so well, Flora proudly says, "She's my All-School Games teacher!"

Children, especially younger children, benefit from having exposure to another teacher during All-School Games. They gain confidence from walking into another classroom and sitting around a new meeting rug, and they grow experientially as they listen to a different teacher relate to children of mixed ages. For young children who might initially find entering a different classroom environment a frightening experience, having older partners eases the transition.

Involvement in All-School Games can also benefit teachers, providing a time to interact with students from many classes. It can provide a time to get acquainted on the playground with children who in a few years will be members of their classroom. These early encounters can ease the transition into new class-rooms particularly for children who struggle with changes. As they watch the different ages play together teachers may enrich their understanding of particular children, noticing aspects which might not be apparent during reading or math. They may see children exhibit sides of themselves rarely displayed when they work in groups with their peers. A child may show surprising compassion for others, a cooperative spirit or a natural talent for leadership. During the games, teachers also enjoy observing how former students have grown and changed. Noting that Ben who had such difficulty sharing his crayons in first grade is so kind to his younger partner may help his teacher maintain a healthier perspective on those difficult days when change seems hard to achieve.

For some young adolescents, playing with younger children gives them permission to briefly let go of some of the posturing and roles maintained in front of their peers and to play uninhibitedly. As they play, friendships which might have otherwise been stymied by artificial barriers are encouraged to grow and flourish.

Jay Lord, a founder of the Center School, recalls a time when children had the opportunity to play with one another across ages every day. At that time the entire school shared the same schedule and then, as now, the school practiced "structured play." In structured play, teachers do not release children onto the playground; instead they organize them into games and activities. Because all of the children were involved in games at the same time, mixed-age games occurred informally everyday. With the growth of the school and the evolution of different daily schedules for different classes, our All-School Games time has had to become carefully planned.

Relationships form during All-School Games which continue
to thrive in the classrooms, hallways and lunchroom.

We continue to make this effort because All-School Games have been very successful. Children love them. Teachers who have over the years built up a repertoire of games that work well across a broad range of ages share their knowledge and help their colleagues learn about their students. Visitors walking around the grounds of Center School during All-School Games time note five-year-old children playing with twelve-year-olds, eight-year-olds with fourteen-year-olds, and so on in an endless array of age combinations, and comment about what a refreshing sight it is. Relationships which form in All-School Games continue to thrive outside the classroom and outside this particular routine. A sense of community develops as children play.

Making All-School Games Safe and Fun for Everyone

Prepare older children for their role as caretakers. Before beginning All-School Games, teachers of the oldest children in the school meet with their students to discuss their role and responsibilities as caretakers for the younger children. Emphasis is placed on understanding how the youngest children might be feeling, especially on the first day, and on helping the youngest children have fun. To encourage empathy, teachers might ask students to recall a time from their younger years when they had to do something that felt scary and involved being with older children, such as starting school, riding on the school bus or participating in All-School Games for the first time. Sharing these stories develops feelings of empathy and sensitizes children to ways in which they can help younger classmates feel more at ease: greeting them warmly, holding their hands, keeping the play gentle, offering encouraging words.

Review signals for attention. Before going on the playground, gather children in a circle and make sure that everyone knows the same signals and understands their purpose. The following signals have worked well for us during outdoor play:

Circle up: When the teacher calls "circle up," players form a circle to wait for the next directions. We also use this call when we notice a problem that needs immediate attention and we want the children to help solve it.

Freeze: When the teacher calls "freeze," players freeze in place.

Hands up: When the players are already in a circle or a line, the teacher raises her hand which signals the players to raise their hands and be silent.

Alee, Alee: This is a call borrowed from Hide and Seek to gather children from anywhere on the playground to a selected spot to hear instructions, discuss a problem that's arisen, or line up to go inside.

Establish a few important rules. There are a few key rules and guidelines which we've found to be very helpful in keeping any outdoor game time safe, fun and friendly.

Giving help: Discuss and practice the specific ways in which players can help each other during a game. For example, what are the procedures to be followed if someone falls down, makes a mistake, feels left out, etc.

Walking, running, and tagging safely: Specifically define and model ways for children to tag each other safely, such as "a gentle tag on the shoulder or back."

Solving conflicts: Create rules which minimize conflicts, particularly around tagging. "Tagger's choice" simply states that the person who is "It" is always right, even if his or her tag was so soft that it wasn't felt by the taggee. This rule has been very helpful in keeping play peaceful and moving along at our school.

Choosing Games for Mixed-Age Groups: Center School Favorites

Here are a few games which we come back to over and over again for our All-School Games. They are safe and fun to play with mixed-ages, they require very little equipment, and the children love them.

Kick the Can

This is a favorite tag game which many teachers remember fondly from their own childhood years. The person who is "It" stands by a tin can in the center of the playing area and counts to ten while everyone else scatters to find hiding places. The object is for someone to kick the can before being spotted by "It." When the child who is "It" spots a player, he/she yells, "I see Karen behind the sandbox one, two, three." "It" must finish this whole sentence before the player gets to the can to kick it. If "It" finishes this call, the player goes to jail (a tree or a step works fine). If the player kicks the can, then that player becomes "It" next. We find that the following rules about jail are helpful: players need to be touching jail at all times or they can be accused of escaping; prisoners get 5 chances to escape for each game; when catching an escaping prisoner, "It" only has to call, "I see you, Sam;" if a prisoner escapes successfully, she has to go to a new hiding place before she can try to kick the can again (that is, no kicking the can from a "hiding place" in jail).

Capture the Flag

This is a strategy game for many. The play area is divided into two sections with lots of room for running. It will look like this:

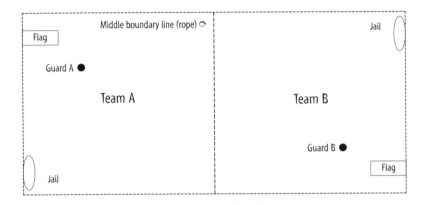

The children are divided evenly into two teams and each team is sent to one side of the play yard. Each team then chooses a guard to watch over their flag and their jail (in very large games in a very large space often there will be two guards—one for the jail and one for the flag). Each team has a flag (a handkerchief or piece of cloth) put in a designated spot and a jail which starts in a designated spot at the end of the play yard.

Objective: To get the other team's flag and bring it back without being tagged by the other team.

Capturing the flag: Children cross over the middle boundary line and try to sneak over to the flag and grab it. If they are tagged by the opposing team, they have to join the jail line which moves out from the jail point towards the middle boundary line. The children in jail must hold hands and each new jail member joins the line at the back. If they are *not* tagged before they get back across the middle boundary line, they are safe. Children venture across the line often without getting the flag.

Points: When a team successfully captures the flag, they receive a point and both teams change sides and appoint new guards.

Guards: The guard is the only one who may stand back by the jail and flag. The guard must stand five giant steps away. Others may chase to the back, but may not stay there. It helps to change guards often and *not* wait for points to change.

Jail: A child can be rescued from jail by a member from his team who reaches the jail line and touches someone in it before being tagged by the opposing team. The rescuer takes the first person in line at the *front* and walking hand in hand over the middle boundary line, they are safe. They must walk hand in hand. If the rescuer gets tagged before reaching the jail line, then he/she must join the end of the jail line.

Parachute Games

You'll find many possibilities for good parachute games to play with mixed ages in *The Second Cooperative Sports & Games Book* (1982) by Terry Orlick, pp. 207–226.

An older child helps her younger buddy
understand the rules of the game.

Silly Soccer

Soccer is a very simple and enjoyable sport for children. Almost every child loves to run and kick and try to score a goal. The trouble, however, especially when playing with mixed ages, is that the faster and stronger usually dominate. To solve this problem, we have created a game which we play a lot during All-School Games called Silly Soccer. It uses the same basic idea of soccer in that competing teams attempt to score a goal by kicking a ball. However, in this version, there are three goals and no traditional soccer rules. The field is in the shape of a triangle with a cone placed at each of the three points of the triangle. These cones serve as the goals as each team attempts to defend their own cone (without the use of an official goalie) while also trying to kick the ball into the other two teams' cones. With three teams and three goals, the game can get quite silly and most players will quickly give up on even trying to keep track of the score and simply enjoy the fun. We find that it works well in this game to have older children partner with younger children, holding hands throughout the play. A ball that's lopsided and rolls in unpredictable ways makes the game even more fun.

Smaug's Jewels

One person is chosen as Smaug, a deadly dragon who stands guard over her jewels (a handkerchief or piece of cloth). Everyone else forms a circle around Smaug and tries to steal the jewels without being tagged. Smaug can range as far from her jewels as she dares. If Smaug tags someone, that person is instantly frozen in place until the end of the game which usually lasts for about a minute.

Captain's Coming

This game is played on a rectangular field, perhaps about 50 feet long and 30 feet wide. The boundaries should be clearly stated but could be as rough as "in line with those trees over there." This game has a number of commands called out in random by the "Captain," the teacher. There is a specific action applied to each command and the last person or few people to perform the act are "out." However, the trick for the captain is to give some of the slower and younger children an advantage by calling out a series of commands before identifying the person who is last. For instance, the captain might call "Land" requiring everyone to run toward the designated land on the far left of the field. Right before they reach the destination (with the older and faster children far in front), the captain calls "Sea" and everyone must turn to run in the opposite direction toward the sea which is on the far right side of the field. Now, the children who were slower to get to the land will have a head start on their trip to the sea.

Commands:

Land: Run to one end of the rectangle

Sea: Run to the other end of the rectangle

Port: Run to one side of rectangle

Starboard: Run to other side of rectangle

Captain's Coming: Line up in the middle of the rectangle facing the captain in saluting position.

Man Overboard: Run to either side of the rectangle looking over the edge.

Abandon Ship: Piggy back with a partner.

Scrub the Decks: Pretend to be scrubbing the decks.

Climb the Rigging: Pretend to climb the rigging.

Relay Races

Divide teams so they are as equal as possible. Align similar speed runners so they are racing against each other. Establish clearly marked starting and turning points (ropes, sticks, fences, chalked lines). Use traditional race formats (running, skipping, hopping on one foot, etc.) or try some of the fun variations we've come up with over the years:

Interaction: the team "operates on" (hugs, shakes hands with, runs two circles around, changes jackets with) a member of their team who stands at the turn around point.

Partner: pairs hold hands, move in a hoop, carry something, clap hands.

Fantasy: children act out stories, animals, jokes, sports as they run.

There are many ways to move: hop, skip, move backwards, roll a ball, kick a ball. Kids will gladly volunteer their notions.

Variety of Tag Games

Tag games are always fun. When playing them with mixed ages, it's important to use a wide variety and to change the game frequently so that everyone enjoys the play. Here are some of our standards:

• *Hug Tag:* Several players are "It." The people being chased can be temporarily safe from being tagged only when they are hugging another player. Each hug should only last for a few seconds. Younger children really enjoy this game.

• *Freeze Tag:* Several children are freezers. When they tag a child, that child freezes in place with his/her legs wide apart. Any other child on the field can attempt to unfreeze this person by crawling through their legs. This can also be played in pairs (partners holding hands) with twin freezers and twin runners.

• *Blob Tag:* One person is chosen to be the Blob. When someone is tagged, he joins hands with the tagger. The Blob grows bigger as more people are caught and continues growing until everyone is one big Blob (or the Blob can split into two Blobs once it becomes eight-people long).

• *Toilet Tag:* When tagged, children freeze in a squatting position like the shape of a toilet, keeping one arm extended into the air until someone unfreezes them by gently pushing their arm down to "flush the toilet."

• *Hospital Tag:* One or two people are "It" and one person is designated as the doctor. When players are tagged, they continue to run around but must put their hand over the place where they were tagged (their wound). When someone has been tagged for the third time, they drop to the ground and call "Doctor, Doctor." The doctor gently touches the person which heals their wounds, allowing them to play again.

Mountain Day

Description: On Mountain Day, our entire school community hikes up the mountain adjacent to Center School for a picnic lunch.

Purpose: The hike takes the children away from the school for a fun hike and a communal lunch experience. Because children hike and eat with their All-School Games group, Mountain Day also provides an opportunity for children of different ages to be together in a fresh context.

Format: Each fall one Center School teacher selects a day based on favorable weather predictions to be "Mountain Day." Once the day has been determined, she informs the staff and students that at 11:30 the next morning everyone will gather to hike up the mountain for lunch. Children hike and eat with their All-School Games group and teacher. Each Mountain Day includes the following components:

- Spontaneity
- A beautiful fall day
- Hiking and eating in mixed-age groups

AT CENTER SCHOOL "Mountain Day" is an annual spontaneous fall event. On this day, children and teachers hike up the mountain behind the school and eat lunch together as a whole-school group. The tradition started in 1989, the first year that Center School was housed in its current building. Inspired by a particularly warm and beautiful fall, the excitement of the new building with its adjacent mountain, and a similar tradition at two nearby colleges, one teacher suggested the idea. It now occurs on a different day each year; yet it always includes the following components: spontaneity; a beautiful fall day; and hiking and eating in mixed-age groups.

Spontaneity

As children arrive at school one day in October, they are treated to a surprise announcement on the morning message chart. It reads: "Good morning everyone! Tomorrow has been chosen as 'Mountain Day.' At 11:30 we will all hike the mountain and eat lunch together in our All-School Games groups. Remember to wear comfortable shoes and bring an appropriate lunch." After reading the chart, children run off to their classrooms chatting excitedly.

A simple walk in the woods offers
many wonderful learning opportunities.

Part of the thrill of Mountain Day is that it always occurs on a beautiful day and its spontaneity surprises everyone, including most of the teachers. A Center School teacher remembers Mountain Day fondly for its impromptu nature. "It's important for children to see that adults can drop their plans for something like this. They see that no plan is so important that it can't be rearranged." Mountain Day is also valuable as a community-builder. This adventure helps children create bonds with each other and with their teachers because of a sense of being "out in the world" together as a whole school. The spirit of adventure helps to make it work by creating excitement for almost everyone.

Hiking in Mixed-Age Groups

Eliza, an eighth grader, wrote about Mountain Day in her journal the next day: "It was an amazing thing to see. At one point I got to the top of a rise where you can see a long way down the trail. There were pairs of kids as far as I could see. Everyone was walking with someone and no one was running ahead or pushing or shoving. Some of the little kids were holding hands with older kids, and some were even being carried on their backs. The trees were hanging over the trail and were all changing colors. I loved it. I didn't think we would be able to do it without driving all the teachers crazy, but they seemed to enjoy it as much as we did."

These partners stop hiking for a moment to look at a caterpillar.

Partners play a game of cat's cradle at "the lunch spot"
while waiting for others to finish eating.

Children hike up the mountain with their All-School Games group and in partners within this group, younger children paired with older children. These partnerships work well in keeping the pace of the hike reasonable for everyone. Younger children set the pace and their older partners adjust their own pace to accommodate their partner's. Hiking within the larger mixed-age groupings also distributes people evenly during the climb. Having children eat and hike in cross-age pairs is a vital part of making Mountain Day work. These pairs help everyone stay in control, while also providing a wonderful opportunity for children to get to know each other. Children share stories of their other hiking adventures, stories of special trees, or stories of the previous day's soccer game. At the clearing known as "the lunch spot" children and teachers gather until all the children have found a spot to eat. A teacher then raises a hand to quiet the group and calls for a moment of silence. This moment—when almost two hundred children and teachers sit together observing the silence and beauty of this place—is memorable.

For teachers another part of the satisfaction of Mountain Day comes from observing how the Center School's structures work when the children are away from the school. They can see whether the children are internalizing their lessons on taking care of one another; observe how they converse with much older or younger children; watch how they follow signals for quiet and for freezing action; and note the way they observe their surroundings.

Although we call our break in routine Mountain Day and hike up a mountain together, the incline is not what is important. A hike to a park or along a nature trail, if it provided a safe place for a whole school outing, would serve the same purpose. The important part is that on Mountain Day we demonstrate our trust by giving children the responsibility of being away from the school as a group and being in control. Though it is a simple and defined adventure, Mountain Day provides plenty of opportunities for children to take care of themselves and others in the woods, to enjoy the pleasure that being out of doors can bring, and to be reminded that "school" is not something that only happens within the confines of our building.

Greetings

Description: At Center School we provide structured opportunities for children and adults within the school to greet each other.

Purpose: Greetings help create and maintain a classroom and school environment that is open and welcoming to all.

Format: Structured greetings take many different forms at Center School, some occurring daily, others weekly or at special junctures once a year. These structures create a school environment that fosters a regular habit of people acknowledging each other. We include structured greetings in

- Morning Meeting
- Back-to-School Conferences
- First Week Greetings

A s WE STRIVE to create a sense of community and connection at the Center School we have come to value greetings for their role in forging bonds and reminding us daily of our communal responsibilities to welcome, include and support our fellow citizens. Greetings establish a friendly and inclusive tone; they allow children to feel known by others; they help children learn names; and they teach children how to make friendly eye contact. Greetings also invite family members to become a part of the community. They help us all feel a little more connected.

Like schools everywhere we greet each other daily with informal "good mornings" between teachers and students. We also engage in more structured greetings during Morning Meeting, at conferences prior to school's opening, and during the first week of school.

Morning Meeting Greetings

"Will you begin the greeting, David?" Today Ms. J. has picked someone to begin silent greeting. David nods and mouths the words, "Good morning, Rebecca" to his classmate across the circle. She mouths, "Good morning, David" and then turns to look around the circle. "Good morning, Alex," she mouths. Alex in turn scans the circle for someone to greet. The room is silent while children give their full attention to watching the greeting, knowing that they will not be able to follow it if they glance away. As it becomes more difficult for the children to find others who have not yet been greeted, the remaining five or six children put their thumbs up to show that they are still waiting. When the last child, Anne, has been greeted she looks back to David. "Good morning, David," she mouths. "Good morning, everyone," David mimes with arms stretched wide.

Kindergartners pass a handshake greeting
around the circle at Morning Meeting.

This greeting is one of many of those that occur during Morning Meeting at our school. Though the silent aspect of this particular greeting is difficult, older children, and even younger children who have become accustomed to the routine of greetings, are able to participate quite successfully. In other Morning Meeting greetings, children might greet each other in a foreign language or toss a ball to a classmate as they say good morning.

Every day in Center School begins with an all-class Morning Meeting in each room and each Morning Meeting includes a structured greeting. This consistency allows each child to know that they will start the day being greeted in a friendly, self-affirming way. Although children may naturally say hello to their friends at school, they don't always extend this welcome to children with whom they feel less comfortable. Structured greetings ensure that whether a student is new to town, perhaps having a hard time finding a social place, or well-ensconced in a secure and popular niche, he or she will start the day named and welcomed—and not just by the teacher. The affirmation provided by beginning the day this way can help children be more open to taking risks in the classroom. They have been noticed and named; they matter. Greetings during Morning Meeting open doorways for interactions to occur more naturally throughout the day. As children become comfortable with new people, they open themselves to opportunities for learning. Teaching children how to greet each other in Morning Meeting fosters a school environment in which children can approach their peers and their teachers in their classrooms, in the hallways, and on the playground more easily.

Favorite Morning Meeting Greetings

Here are a few favorite greetings from teachers of primary and middle grades to add to or begin your repertoire. As children become familiar with the greeting ritual, they will start to make adaptations to favorite greetings and bring in new ideas of their own.

Simple Greetings for All Ages

"Good Morning _____."
• simple face to face

- with handshake
- with "high five"
- with a hug
- with a touch on the shoulder
- with a wave

Farmer in the Dell Greeting

A group of 2nd and 3rd grade teachers from a school in Washington, DC shared this greeting as a favorite in their classrooms:

To the tune of *Farmer in the Dell*

All the children sing:

(Fill in the child's name) is here, _____ is here.
It's a great day because _____ is here.

Energetic six year olds enjoy the clapping and singing
in this favorite "Farmer in the Dell" greeting.

All the children are seated in their circle. Tammy, who starts the greeting stands up. She offers a handshake to Jeremy who is sitting next to her. Jeremy stands up to receive the handshake. At the same time that Tammy offers her handshake to Jeremy, the rest of the class starts to sing the song using Jeremy's name (Jeremy is here, Jeremy is here...). During the singing of the second line (It's a great day...) everyone claps their hands in rhythm to the tune. Tammy and Jeremy remain standing while Jeremy then offers a handshake to the next child. It continues until everyone is standing and the song comes back to Tammy, who is the last individual greeted. The greeting closes with everyone clapping and singing. "We all are here. We all are here. It's a great day because we all are here!"

Ball Toss Greetings

Arona McNeil-Vann, a K–1 teacher in Washington, DC likes this greeting because it's physical and it encourages the children to greet someone who's not sitting next to them.

Each child greets another child, then gently throws or rolls a ball (nerf ball, beach ball, sponge ball) underhand to that child who in turn greets back. The greeting ends when the ball returns to the starter.

Ball Toss Variations for Middle Grades

Jane Stephenson and Beth Watrous, teachers at Greenfield Center School, offer these variations for use in the middle grades (4–6) and older to make it more challenging and to build coop- eration between older children:

• After the initial ball toss, students send the ball on a second round silently (with no greeting or talking) repeating the pattern just made. Children will enjoy doing it several times this way and competing against the clock.

• Begin the first ball silently and at even intervals add one or two more balls so that there are several balls going around in the pattern in which children greeted one another. Challenge the children to see if they can do it three times, without dropping and know exactly where to stop. You can also add the element of competition against the clock.

- Once the greeting ball has finished its first cycle, have the children "undo the greeting pattern" by sending the ball back to the person who greeted them. They can attach a greeting or pass the ball silently. When the children get very good at remembering who greeted them, try ending Morning Meeting with a ball toss in the reverse greeting pattern as they wish each other, "Have a good working day!" or other encouraging words the children decide they want to say that day.

Name Card Greeting

Tim Keefe, a fifth grade teacher in West Haven, Connecticut likes to keep greetings "simple and sincere." At the beginning of the year, he finds that the Name Card Greeting works particularly well because it helps the students learn each other's names and it allows them to greet different students each day.

Place a stack of student name cards in the center of your circle. The first person chooses the top card from the pile and greets that person.

Back-to-School Conferences

When Isabelle and her mom, Janice, walk into the third grade classroom with its recently polished floor and its cans full of new markers and perfectly sharpened pencils, Isabelle is very nervous. She is clutching her mom's hand and seems reluctant to take her seat across the table from her new teacher. "Hello, Isabelle, hello, Janice." Ms. D., who has had hundreds of these conferences over her years at Center School, knows how to make children feel comfortable with their new classroom and teacher. She bends down toward Isabelle. "How are you? Can you tell me one thing that you did this summer?" Once Isabelle feels more relaxed, Ms. D. begins to tell her about what the third graders will be doing during the first week of school.

These conferences occur each August at Center School. They serve as a way to welcome children and their parents to their new classroom, introduce them to their new teachers, and give them a chance to share their hopes and dreams for the year. Parents are invited to share any concerns that they may have with the new teacher and to discuss what sort of role they wish to play in their child's year at school. By helping teachers learn more about their new students and by allowing children to acclimate to their new classroom before they arrive for the first day of school, Back-to-School Conferences reduce some of the confusion and anxiety that can otherwise accompany opening day.

Welcome Back Ice-Cream Social.

One Center School teacher who taught for a year at an elementary school in a neighboring town upheld the tradition of hosting Back-to-School conferences. She had done this for years at Center School, and even though no other teacher at her new school held conferences prior to the opening of school, she thought them vital to having a good start to the year: "The thought of starting school without knowing these children at all is too overwhelming. The conferences take a lot of time and energy but they're worth it in the end." Many teachers at Center School agree that these conferences are labor intensive; yet their value makes the effort worthwhile. Attending to important business, welcoming parents and students, and ensuring a sense of belonging all serve to ease the transition back to school for students, parents and teachers.

A teacher welcomes a parent into the classroom
at a Back-to-School Conference.

First Week Greetings

"Here comes someone I don't recognize," Michael says to his sixth grade classmate Ellen as he moves to approach the frightened looking kindergartner. "My name is Michael and I'm going to show you where your new classroom is. Which class are you in?" Colin, a brand new kindergartner, shyly whispers, "Prime Reds." Michael takes Colin's hand and leads him up the stairs to his classroom. Colin's parents, equally nervous about this momentous occasion, exchange smiles as they watch Colin accompany his escort and they follow the two upstairs.

Use older
Students as
Greeters (Student
Council) -
Conferences
Assemblies
School Events

Michael is what is known at Center School as a "greeter," a sixth grader who agrees to welcome new kindergartners to school by helping them find their classrooms during the first week of school. Greeters stand in front of the doors to the school and watch for new students. When they see children whom they do not recognize they approach them with a hello and an offer to escort them to their new classroom.

Greeters provide a vital service to new students. By greeting them with a friendly hello and providing a point of contact, they help ease the transition into a foreign environment. Selection as a student greeter may also provide an important transition for the greeter. Being chosen involves honor and pride and many sixth graders aspire to the role. Teachers choose greeters with care, nominating students who will thrive on the responsibility of a serious job and who have demonstrated warmth and kindness. They are not necessarily those who shine easily at academics. While not all sixth graders are eager to do this job, selection can mark the turning point for a child who has previously escaped recognition or who has perhaps received his recognition from less positive actions.

Student greeters also provide a service to parents, weaning them gently from their role as chief caretaker. As the students welcome the child with warmth and friendliness, they demonstrate to the parents through their actions that the school contains many people, teachers and students, who care about and take responsibility for each other.

Greeting in this way requires the sixth graders to reach back and remember their own entry into school, perhaps calling also upon more recent moments when they were newcomers somewhere—summer camp or swim team. And as they stand for a figurative moment in the small, new-for-the-first-week-of-school sneakers of their young partners, they draw upon compassion and act with empathy.

Feeling Welcome

Greetings are consciously woven in this way through every aspect of life in the school. They take place daily at Morning Meeting, weekly at All-School Meeting, and yearly at Back-to-School Conferences and during the first week of school. The pleasure of being part of a community in which people acknowledge and welcome each other and the habits that inevitably grow from these structures teach children the importance of greeting others.

There is a general tone at Center School of feeling welcome. The deliberate actions that establish an expectation of greetings within the school spill over and produce informal greetings among children and adults throughout the day. One teacher who was new to Center School exclaimed about this feeling one day during her first week at the school, after spending over twenty years teaching in a nearby school community. After being greeted with "good morning" by at least three teachers on her way into a staff meeting, she remarked, "I can't believe how welcoming everyone here is! At my old school you could get away with walking into a meeting and burying your head in your papers without acknowledging anyone. It's such a nice feeling not to be able to get away with that."

First Week Greetings
tied into CARE Program .

49

The Magic Penny Ceremony

Description: During the Magic Penny Ceremony the Center School community gathers together to say goodbye and present a gift of a "magic penny" to staff members leaving the school and to students leaving the school before eighth grade graduation.

Purpose: This ceremony acknowledges the accomplishments of students and staff leaving Center School and allows the community to say farewell.

Format: Teachers read speeches which honor the accomplishments and experiences of students and staff members who are leaving. Each individual is celebrated in turn and given a "magic penny" by someone important to them. At the end of the ceremony, the "Magic Penny" song is sung. If a student or staff member leaves Center School mid-year the ceremony takes place during All-School Meeting. Each Magic Penny Ceremony includes the following components:

- Entrance songs
- Speeches honoring students and staff
- The "magic penny" presentation
- The "Magic Penny" song
- Departure songs

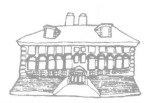

THE MAGIC PENNY CEREMONY, like All-School Meeting, is a tradition that came to Center School from the Gill Elementary School in Gill, MA. The teachers who introduced it to the school believed children and adults both needed support during transitions and valued this ceremony as a formal way to give students and staff that support as they say farewell to members of the community.

During the ceremony students who leave Center School before they reach eighth grade receive a "magic penny," a newly minted penny that is given as a gift in a special case. Staff who leave the school also receive a penny. The penny acknowledges and celebrates their participation in our community as students, teachers, friends, or acquaintances. The ceremony includes the Center School community, parents, and the following components: speeches for students; speeches for staff members; the presentation of the magic penny; and singing.

Speeches for Students

"When we think of Samantha we'll always remember her flying down the soccer field, wildly cheering on her teammates as she deftly passes the ball. Samantha will be greatly missed at Center School for her positive spirit and willing support of others. She has been a role model for us all." While her teacher delivers this speech, Samantha scans through the audience and catches glances from some of her classmates. Samantha's parents and her aunt sit proudly listening.

Speeches briefly highlight something special about the child who is leaving so that the child may depart from the community feeling acknowledged and self-confident. The ceremony was designed not to mimic graduation but to offer a small ceremony that recognizes an important transition for children. Though the speeches are shorter and less elaborate than at graduation, the ceremony nevertheless offers a chance to celebrate a child's accomplishments in front of the school community and provides a rite of passage for children as they depart.

The "Magic Penny" Presentation

As her teacher finishes up Samantha's speech and gives her a hug, Samantha sees her best friend Kim getting up from her seat and coming toward the stage. When Kim reaches the edge of the stage she hops up and hands Samantha her "magic penny." Samantha gives her a hug and together they jump off the stage and race back to their seats. They are nervous and giggly as they sit down. While the next child and teacher take the stage Samantha closely examines her penny.

Children play a key role in the ceremony. A special friend, often someone considered to be a "best friend," presents the penny. Teachers prepare the presenting children for their role beforehand and give them the penny to hold quietly during the ceremony. They convey the idea that both the penny and the ceremony are special occasions for children who are leaving Center School and children treat their role seriously.

Speeches for Staff

Ms. W. is called on to the stage after the last departing student has received his penny. She is the first of three staff members honored in this year's ceremony. Rather than the typical speech read by one person, this speech looks a bit different. Six teachers stand on the stage holding huge sheets of poster board behind their backs. The children in the audience are whispering excitedly.

When everyone is quiet, the teacher on the left holds up his poster. It says "J." The second teacher holds hers up. It says "O." They continue until they have spelled "JOANNE" across the stage. The teacher on the left begins by saying "jovial." The next teacher says "optimistic." The third says "atypical." The fourth says "nifty." They go on and on, each teacher pronouncing five adjectives in all that begin with the letter that he or she is holding up. When they are through they take a bow and motion for Ms. W. to take a bow as the crowd roars with applause. They each hug her and step off the stage.

Sometimes, the speeches for staff members have a lighter tone than those for students. Their leaving is taken seriously; yet we also feel that a lighthearted presentation can make their departure easier for children to accept. Often, after listening to many speeches for students, the youngest children are ready for some humor and improvisation on the part of their teachers. Children may feel sad that their teachers are leaving and have trouble understanding why the departure is necessary. A lighthearted speech, while not always necessary or suitable for a staff member, can help to ease this burden for children.

Staff members lead the community in singing the "Magic Penny" song.

The "Magic Penny" Song

After the last staff member has stepped down from the stage, staff members who are sitting at the front with their guitars begin singing the song, "Magic Penny." Soon the whole crowd joins in.

At this ceremony, as in all Center School ceremonies, singing plays a central role. Everyone knows the songs—students, staff, and parents—and we sing with enthusiasm. After singing the "magic penny" song and honoring the students and staff who are leaving, we continue to sing. Since the ceremony usually occurs on the day before graduation, we have graduation songs to practice and voices to warm for the next ceremony. One of the school's founders often leads the crowd in singing songs from the school repertoire.

Children at our school, like children everywhere, look forward to graduation from eighth grade as the culmination of their experience at the Center School. Having to leave before eighth grade and not getting to be part of this important day can be difficult for some children. The Magic Penny Ceremony helps to alleviate some of this disappointment and provides an opportunity to enjoy a "moment in the sun" similar to a graduation.

Some Ceremony Essentials

Singing

Singing has become an essential ingredient of this ceremony. We sing a coming-in and going-out song as well as the "Magic Penny" song (*Rise Up Singing,* p. 240) after the last farewell speech. At the end of the ceremony, we also take 15 minutes to practice songs for graduation which is held the following day. We usually have a few staff members (and occasionally an older student) who play guitar and lead us in our singing.

The Magic Penny

The "magic pennies" which the children and staff members receive during the ceremony are newly minted pennies which we place in a plastic coin case. We order the cases through our local coin shop.

Setting

We generally hold this ceremony outdoors—under a tent—to add to the out-of-the-ordinary feeling, to accommodate the parents who wish to attend, and to take advantage of our lovely June New England weather.

Graduation

Description: Graduation at Center School is a rite of passage. The ceremony is held on the last day of school and celebrates the accomplishments of the eighth graders. All students attend and all community members are invited.

Purpose: This ceremony acknowledges the hard work of graduates and marks their passage into high school. The ceremony also honors parents whose children are graduating.

Format: At graduation the entire school participates in a ceremony of songs, speeches, and stories. Parents read the story of "Horse," a Center School folktale; seventh and eighth grade teachers read speeches about each individual graduate; staff members sing to graduates; and graduates present the school with a class gift. The Graduation Ceremony always includes the following components:

- The story of "Horse"
- Speeches
- Songs
- A class gift

THE CENTER SCHOOL GRADUATION CEREMONY has changed little from the first celebration of three eighth graders to the most recent graduation of twenty-five students. It remains a special way to mark the passage of children into the world of high school. The ceremony is structured both to acknowledge and honor each graduate's special qualities and to allow the seventh and eighth grade teachers, other staff members, and students a chance to say goodbye to the graduates, the graduates a chance to say goodbye to Center School, and the parents a chance to participate in their child's graduation.

The ceremony consists of the following components: a reading of the story of "Horse;" speeches honoring graduates; a staff song for graduates; and the presentation of a gift from the eighth graders to the school.

The Story of "Horse"

Well, it happened that Horse was leading Fox, Dog, Rat, Sheep, Goat and other gentle beasts from the old forest to the new. It had been a long winter, but the day was grand and Horse pranced along, his mane flying in the wind, as if a flag-bearer. At times, the shorter-legged creatures would climb aboard his back and rest when weary as the procession continued. Suddenly they came to a rushing river. Across the river there fell a log. The log was just long enough, narrow enough and high enough to need careful feet to cross safely. Horse was first and he stepped up. No sooner did he have all fours on the log than he was filled with dread. Suppose he slipped? Suppose he lost his balance and fell over? Suppose the log began to shake with his weight?. . .

"Horse" was written by Greenfield Center School co-founder Ruth Charney before the Center School opened in 1981. (For the complete story of "Horse," see the Appendix on page 69.) It helps prepare children for their most difficult journeys and to encourage them to persist, even when frightened or discouraged. It is a story about getting from old to new with the help of others, a fitting story for children in transition. Originally read by Ruth, it now is read by the parents who are leaving the Center School community with the graduation of their eighth grader. Each parent stands on stage and approaches the microphone in turn to read a segment of the story. This opportunity to participate in the ceremony also acknowledges their own passage.

Parent involvement is very important at the Center School. Parents play key roles in chaperoning field trips and in organizing events. In order to encourage good communication between families and teachers, parents and teachers keep in very close contact. This leads to a strong sense of familiarity for many parents who become recognized and known by many students and teachers. Inviting parents to participate acknowledges their role in supporting and nourishing both their own child's growth and development as a student and that of other children in the school through their participation in school activities.

The graduating eighth grader stands right next to his teacher
during the presentation of the graduation speech.

Speeches

*After the parents have finished reading the story of "Horse," they
return to their seats amidst the loud cheering of the graduates.
Many enjoy seeing their parents on stage. Ms. F., an eighth grade
teacher, takes the stage and calls Elana to the stage. She is the first
eighth grader to receive her ring and to be honored. Ms. F. begins
her speech with Elana standing close beside her: "I have known
Elana since she was a kindergartner but it wasn't until she
became a seventh grader that I became her teacher. Over the last
two years, I have seen her grow into a confident and clever young
woman."*

The graduation speeches, personal and touching to students,
teachers, and parents, let graduates know how well their teachers have understood them. Each student is addressed by one
teacher from the seventh-eighth grade team, a teacher who has
grown to know that particular student well. These speeches
reflect the strong connections between teachers and students in
the classroom.

During the speeches each graduate hears the importance of his or her experience at Center School shared with the entire school community. Often the speeches contain funny moments as teachers recall their favorite memories. Sometimes there is a sad moment as a teacher reflects on the graduate's particular struggles during his or her last two years at the school. Hearing the stories of their elementary school moments brings a certain closure as children prepare to turn toward the new experience of high school.

The Staff Song

Midway through the speeches, staff members begin to take the stage for the traditional "staff song." They approach the stage with some nervousness over the prospect of singing in front of so many people. After a few moments with the group of approximately forty staff members finally arranged on the stage, the teachers who play guitar begin strumming and the staff joins in singing, "Take Time Young Eaglets." This is a song which Center School co-founder Chip Wood wrote specifically for Graduation. It is an adaptation of a traditional Irish song called "The Castle of Dromore."

. . . Take time to thrive, our rays of hope
  In this garden by the door
  Take heed young eaglets till thy wings
  Are feathered fit to soar
  A little rest, and then the world
  Is full of work to do
    Singing hush a bye loo, low loo low lan
    Hush a bye loo, low loo
(from "Take Time Young Eaglets")

Through this song, staff members say farewell to the graduates, some of whom they have known for many years. In addition to the staff song, the community sings many other songs which are familiar from All-School Meetings and special events. All of the songs touch on the same themes as the story of "Horse": helping one another and moving on.

During graduation we continue the tradition of singing which is a central part of Center School life. Most students, staff members, and parents know the songs by heart. After the staff song the teachers present more graduates with rings and speeches. Speeches are interspersed with singing throughout the ceremony.

The Class Gift Presentation

When the last speech is completed and the last Center School graduate has taken her seat, three representatives from the graduating class take the stage. They approach the microphone with both trepidation and big smiles as they figure out at what distance they need to stand in order to be heard. It is quite a windy June day and they want to be sure that everyone can hear them.

Clare begins, "We have been raising money to buy the Center School a gift. We have been searching high and low trying to find something that you all can remember us by." Steven continues, "We think that we finally did it. We know that our gift will eventually grow larger than us and will live on at the Center School after most of us are gone." Hashim concludes the presentation, "We have planted two trees on the Center School grounds. One is to represent our graduating class, and one is to represent Ms. P. who was a teacher for most of us at one point or another and who is leaving Center School this year. We will miss her and we will miss the Center School."

Each year the graduates work hard to choose a gift that will both represent them long after they are gone and be something either useful or beautiful for the school community. In this recent example, the graduates took care to choose something that would remain beautiful and carry meaning for many years.

A Tribute to the Graduates

"One of the greatest parts of our ceremony," recalls Director Jay Lord, "is that the graduates get to leave the school feeling as if they are really known by everyone. And they are." Jay's statement sums up one of the most distinct parts of the Center School Graduation Ceremony. The speeches are a tribute to hard work and are a way of showing graduates that we recognize and appreciate their achievements. We wish them well while also addressing each individual's unique qualities. The speeches are personal, detailing specific accomplishments, and the graduates cherish them.

Graduation is also a meaningful ceremony for the students remaining at Center School. Many of the eighth graders have become well known to younger children through their presentations in All-School Meetings, their work as greeters, their partnerships in playing All-School Games, and their general presence throughout the school community. Through many of these functions, they evolve into role models, admired and respected by children of all ages. As the younger children sit listening during the long ceremony, many enjoy being able to watch their older friends graduate and perhaps dream briefly about their own graduation to come.

Making Graduation Special

The Songs

As with our other ceremonies, singing is an important part of Graduation. We sing the same songs year after year, songs which have been selected specifically for this ceremony and which we generally do not sing at other times in the school year. These are songs which are "saved" for graduation adding to specialness of this ceremony. Here are the songs we have chosen:

Love Will Guide Us (*Rise Up Singing,* p. 118)

Vine and Fig Tree (*Rise Up Singing,* p. 198)

Take Time Young Eaglets (Chip Wood's adaptation of a traditional Irish song called "The Castle of Dromore")

Love From the Center School (This is also a song which Chip Wood created for Center School Graduation. It is an adaptation of Gordon Bok's song, "Hearth and Fire" which can be found in *Rise Up Singing,* p. 109.)

The Setting

As with the Magic Penny ceremony, we generally hold Graduation under a tent outdoors. Graduation is scheduled for the day after the Magic Penny Ceremony so that we can use the same tent. There are folding chairs for students, staff, parents and friends with a central aisle for the graduates to enter. We use a platform stage and a microphone so that everyone in the audience can see the graduates and hear the speeches.

The Flowers

A few days before graduation, a note is sent to all staff and parents requesting flowers from their gardens to make the stage area and the seating area for the graduates beautiful and festive.

The Rings

We buy a simple silver band from a local jeweler for every graduate. At the end of the graduation speech, a close friend or sibling carries the ring to the graduate on stage.

Conclusion
A Gift from the Students

An older student listens to his younger partner's stories
during a Tuesday lunch.

LAST YEAR a new program, the Tuesday Lunch Program, was begun at the Center School. The Tuesday Lunch Program is not a Center School tradition, though it may become one. It arose not from an intention to create another tradition, but rather out of an attempt to solve a community problem. Assistant teachers and part-time staff usually left at mid-day and were therefore inadvertently excluded from staff meetings scheduled after school. We wanted a way to meet when the entire staff could be present. The idea to have students monitor the lunches so staff could meet during the meal time was suggested almost in jest at first, but it turned into a workable solution to our problem. It is included here because it suggests another dimension to the role of traditions. We were able to solve a knotty problem within our community by drawing upon the resources within that community. It succeeded at least partly because of the wealth of common signals and routines, expectations and values embedded in the traditions which already permeated life at our school. It was a program that had its snags and bad moments, but by and large it worked. One hundred eighty children were kept safe; lunch and quiet time happened quite reasonably; and the entire school staff was able to meet. In the end, it was a gift from the students.

Meg, an eighth-grader, stands at the front of the classroom while children enter the room. When everyone has arrived and is seated she rings the classroom bell, the school-wide signal for quiet. The children quiet and give Meg their attention as she announces that they will eat lunch after a moment of silence. "Let it begin," says Meg. The room is silent. Pairs of older and younger children ranging in age from five to fourteen sit quietly, lunch boxes before them on the table. One kindergartner begins to whisper to his friend across the table; his sixth grade partner quickly quiets him and again the room is silent. After what she considers an acceptable amount of time, Meg decides that lunch may begin: "Have a good lunch," she says.

The children begin to eat and chat with one another. Their conversations cover a broad range of topics from what's inside their lunches to talk of favorite colors, favorite animals, best friends, and brothers and sisters. It is primarily the job of the older partners to keep conversation flowing along.

Because children eat lunch in classrooms at Center School (there is no cafeteria), they are accustomed to this lunch environment; and because lunch rules are universal at the school, there is no confusion about what they can and cannot do during the lunch program. Children know the rules. They know that they may talk to their partners and others at their table, but that they may not talk across tables. They know that they must stay seated during lunch. They know that when lunch is over they must all choose a job to do at their table. They know that lunch is a time for discussion, not reading, drawing, or playing cards. For the most part they abide by these rules.

Meg's lunch program runs smoothly today. When James spills his juice, his fifth grade partner, Kristen, helps him clean it up. When five-year-old Matt begins to wander over to the fish tank, his partner redirects him to the table.

After about twenty minutes, Meg again rings the bell and announces that it is time to clean up. The children at each individual table quickly select their jobs. "I'll be washer," Sarah says. "I'll dry," says her second grade partner, Kevin. "I'll sweep the floor," pipes in Craig. Craig looks to his first grade partner, Simon, who has not yet taken a job. "Why don't you push in the chairs, Simon?" he suggests. "Okay," Simon says, relieved by the assignment. The room is abuzz with the activity of the children cleaning up their tables.

As they finish their clean up jobs, the children begin to scatter about the room with their partners in search of a place to sit for quiet time. Meg walks about the room checking tables and helping

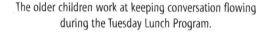

The older children work at keeping conversation flowing during the Tuesday Lunch Program.

64

children find comfortable places to sit in this unfamiliar room. As they settle in, Meg again makes her way to the classroom bell. It takes only seconds for the room to quiet after she rings it. "Quiet time is beginning," she announces. The room is silent.

All around the school, individual rooms fall quiet. The halls are silent. Children are reading, doing math homework, drawing. Some of the young children relax on mats. Some of the older children are helping their younger partners get settled with their quiet time activity.

Meanwhile, across the school yard the Center School teaching staff is meeting. Four parent volunteers wait in the hallways and school tutoring room, on hand in case of an emergency, but today they haven't been needed by the children.

At one o'clock, Meg rings the bell for the last time at this week's lunch program. "Quiet time is over. You can go back to your classrooms," she announces. After the older children escort their younger partners back to their classrooms, they go back to their own rooms where their teachers are waiting for them.

The Tuesday Lunch Program was possible in large part because the older children accepted the responsibility in spite of the difficulties involved. Tied by common bonds forged through daily practices of caring for each other, they wanted to help solve our communal problem. We cautioned them at the outset that it wouldn't necessarily be easy or fun or come with tangible rewards. Most important, it would only work if they were serious and committed. The older students were committed, and their commitment helped them hang on during the times it was less than fun, when problems such as younger children challenging older students' authority arose. Sometimes they really, really wanted to be doing something else. However, it was something more than commitment, important as that was, that enabled their accomplishment. They were well prepared and well supported when troubles erupted. They knew what to do because they had been taking on bits and pieces all along. They, better than anyone, knew the drills. Most of the older children were peer-tutors, greeters, lunch assistants and game leaders. And it was also helpful that, given the familiar routines and expectations, the younger children also knew what they had to do and also wished to help solve our problem.

We do not know yet if the Tuesday Lunch Program will be continued. The problem of the staff meeting schedule has been largely solved through other organizational changes. In order for this particular practice to grow into tradition, different purposes which it serves must be identified. For we have learned that traditions without purpose are hollow and do not—in fact, should not—last.

Perhaps this program—students taking care of themselves without adult supervision in the room—is a meaningful next step for our students' sense of belonging and responsibility. Can we make time and take care to reinforce and encourage the learning and constructive problem-solving that are needed to help the program run well? Will the children feel the same commitment if there isn't the concrete reality of a problem that they are helping to solve?

We must constantly examine and reexamine our traditions. They must have purpose; they must make sense; and they must be sustainable within the constraints of our resources of time and energy. When these measures are met, traditions allow us to pass on what we know and what we care about. At Center School we have built our traditions around creating and sustaining a sense of community and meeting the most vital needs of that community.

But we must remember that schools are, like all human communities, dynamic organisms. The community whose needs we are meeting doesn't get defined once and tidily stay that way. Some changes are predictable and foreseen; others swoop upon us. New students enter in September; returning students bring new experiences and issues with them. A beloved staff member retires; a new teacher takes her place. Fire claims the home of another student and the life of his father. Compassion and sympathy and, yes, a sense of jeopardy, fill the hallway air. The paper factory closes and several parents are unemployed. A major street in town is refurbished and a bikeway for which the school helped petition and clear brush is constructed. Its opening is marked by celebration—a parade of bikes, and tricycles festooned with crepe paper streamers. The mix of people, events, and the texture of the larger environment in which we live shifts and swirls and reminds us that change is a constant. Sometimes we welcome it, and sometimes we resist. But change is inevitable.

It is tempting, sometimes, to view traditions as a way to deny change or to retreat from the disequilibrium that change brings. And certainly the comfort that traditions offer with their predictable and familiar elements is important. But we have come to view the importance of our strongest traditions through a wider lens. The fundamental common ground they provide allows us the potential for continuity in the face of the constant and inevitable change that is a hallmark of school life. Our best traditions do not let us deny or retreat from change; they empower us to deal with it.

About the Author

Libby Woodfin currently teaches in a combined 5th/6th grade classroom at Greenfield Center School. She graduated from Hampshire College in Amherst, Massachusetts where her studies focused on the role of personal stories and histories in education. Libby has also worked as a special needs tutor and has assisted at Northeast Foundation for Children workshops. She lives in Deerfield, Massachusetts.

Appendix
Horse

By Ruth Sidney Charney

THIS STORY I'M ABOUT TO TELL YOU is mostly true, though since it happened more than a week ago it may have come into some changes. I shall tell you what I heard.

Well, it happened that Horse was leading Fox, Dog, Rat, Sheep, Goat and other gentle beasts from the old forest to the new. It had been a long winter, but the day was grand and Horse pranced along, his mane flying in the wind, as if a flag-bearer. At times, the shorter-legged creatures would climb aboard his back and rest when weary as the procession continued. Suddenly they came to a rushing river. Across the river there fell a log. The log was just long enough, narrow enough and high enough to need careful feet to cross safely. Horse was first and he stepped up. No sooner did he have all fours on the log than he was filled with dread. Suppose he slipped? Suppose he lost his balance and fell over? Suppose the log began to shake with his weight? Horse backed off the log. He turned to Goat and ordered, "You are lighter. You go first." Goat was nimble, a climber of steep cliffs. He was over the log in no time. Even Donkey did not pause or ponder. He swayed a bit, his hind quarters seeming to go on their crooked way apart from his fore quarters, but soon he too was across. And then there was only Horse. He considered swimming the river. The current looked swift; the waters were icy. There was no telling where he would end up or if he would end up. Now the others were waiting. Horse could not go forward or backward. Could he stop here and make this his new settlement? He knew there were better places ahead. Could he go back to the old place? There wasn't much food left. He would not—could not go on. While he stood still in uncertainty

and fear, the other animals were meeting.

"Horse has left us," cried Rabbit.

"Horse doesn't like us," said Sheep.

"Horse has found the best spot and wants to keep it for himself," said Turtle.

"Horse is scared stiff," said Beaver.

Horse scared? The other animals couldn't imagine it! What is he scared of? It couldn't be that something they accomplished would trouble the fast and strong Horse.

"Perhaps," murmured Mouse, "a monster lurks in the depths of the river and only Horse knows. He let us almost die," thought Mouse bitterly.

So for the next long time all the animals stood still and watched Horse being scared. Finally after a forever long time, Fox cried out, "Horse? Are you thinking?" And Horse said, "Yes."

"What—if I may ask—are you thinking about?" said Fox.

Horse answered, "The log."

Fox said, "The log? What about the log, Horse?"

Horse sighed, "Why must a log be round on all sides, Fox?"

Fox replied, "Round it is, Horse."

Horse: "I was thinking it would be better to make logs flat."

Then Rat piped up, "Horse are you coming or staying?"

Horse said in a soft voice, not at all usual for him, "I would come—if I could come—but I can't come."

And Beaver repeated, "He's scared stiff."

So the animals stood silent for a while more and watched Horse being scared on the far shore. Then a creature who had not yet spoken said, "Let's help Horse cross the log."

The other beasts opened their eyes as wide as possible and grinned a most incredulous grin. "We cannot pull Horse. We cannot push Horse." And the small but knowing creature said wisely, "We can keep him company."

So all the animals, big and small, sure and awkward of foot, returned across the log. They explained the plan to Horse. Then all lined up. Donkey, seeing Horse tremble a bit, went over and said in a quiet tone so only Horse should hear, "Just pay attention Horse to what's most important." "What's that, Donkey?" said Horse. "To keep going," said Donkey.

And so it happened that there was a trail across the log and Horse was in the middle, Fox holding his tail from behind and Horse holding Goat's stub of a tail in front. Slow and slower and pause and slow they marched until each and every animal crossed the log. Safely.

And that is—from what I heard—how it came to be that the animals came to the new forest where they have been for some time now. Which goes to show that there is always some point, often along the most important journeys, where fear is great and the best care from others helps us make it. And, perhaps *we* must also remember to pay attention to what's most important.

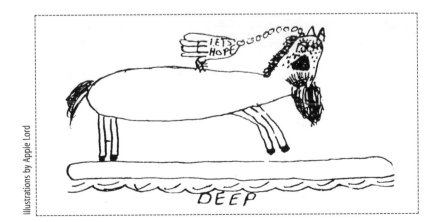

Illustrations by Apple Lord

References

Beall, P.C. and S.H. Nipp. 1982. *Wee Sing Silly Songs.* Los Angeles, CA: Price, Stern & Sloan.

Blood, P. and A. Patterson (Eds.). 1992. *Rise Up Singing: The Group Singing Songbook.* Bethlehem, PA: A Sing Out Publication.*

Cassidy, Nancy and John. 1988. *The Books of Kids' Songs.* Palo Alto, CA: Klutz Press.

Luvmour, Sambhava and Josette. 1990. *Everyone Wins! Cooperative Games and Activities.* Philadelphia, PA and Gabriola Island, BC: New Society Publishers.*

Orlick, Terry. 1978. *The Cooperative Sports & Games Book.* New York: Pantheon Books.*

Orlick, Terry. 1982. *The Second Cooperative Sports & Games Book.* New York: Pantheon Books.*

Silber, Irwin and Fred (Eds.). 1973. *Folksinger's Wordbook.* New York: Oak Publications.

These books are available from Northeast Foundation for Children, 1-800-360-6332.

Additional Teacher Resources from Northeast Foundation for Children

Off to a Good Start: Launching the School Year
Excerpts from the Responsive Classroom Newsletter

The first book in The Responsive Classroom Series features many ideas for building a strong and caring classroom community. 72 pages

Habits of Goodness: Case Studies in the Social Curriculum
by Ruth Sidney Charney

Six elementary school teachers study problems from their classroom concerning the social curriculum. 196 pages

Teaching Children to Care: Management in the Responsive Classroom
by Ruth Sidney Charney

Offers practical approaches for bringing the practice of caring into K–8 classrooms. 309 pages

Yardsticks: Children in the Classroom, Ages 4–14
by Chip Wood

User-friendly guidebook with clear and concise descriptions of developmental stages of children. 228 pages

On Their Side: Helping Children Take Charge of Their Learning
by Bob Strachota

An elementary school teacher shares strategies for helping children invest in their learning. 160 pages

A Notebook for Teachers: Making Changes in the Elementary Curriculum
by Northeast Foundation for Children Staff

Ideas for creating a developmentally appropriate classroom curriculum and environment for 5, 6 and 7 year olds. 79 pages

Places to Start: Implementing the Developmental Classroom
by Marlynn K. Clayton

This video offers a wealth of ideas for creating active and caring classroom communities, K–3. 90 minutes

For Ordering Information

Call 1-800-360-6332